Hardwood Heroes

by John Smallwood

SCHOLASTIC INC.

New York   Toronto   London   Auckland   Sydney
Mexico City   New Delhi   Hong Kong   Buenos Aires

ISBN 0-439-78804-8

12   11   10   9   8   7   6   5   4   3   2   6   7   8   9   10/0

Printed in the U.S.A.
First Scholastic printing, January 2006

The tears were still flowing when Gilbert Arenas finally heard his name called. After averaging 15.7 points in 70 games at the University of Arizona, Gilbert was convinced he would be a first-round pick, so he left school after his sophomore season to enter the 2001 NBA Draft.

But Gilbert didn't get selected until the second round by the Golden State Warriors. "As a player leaving early, you always look back and wonder what could have been," said Gilbert. "But you have to be happy with your decisions, because you ultimately have to live with them."

Gilbert didn't make the instant impact he wanted. It wasn't until he was asked to take over as point guard, a position he had never really played, that his career blossomed.

Despite starting just 30 games, Gilbert finished fourth in scoring and third in assists and steals among rookies. The next season, he started 82 games and averaged 18.1 points and 6.7 assists. Because he was a second-round pick, Gilbert became a free agent after just two seasons. To decide between offers by the Washington Wizards and Los Angeles Clippers, he flipped a coin 10 times. The Wizards won.

Gilbert brought some odd quirks to Washington. He is a practical joker, but his out-of-season workouts are some of the toughest in basketball. He eats at the same restaurant before games, dresses in the same order, and listens to the same songs in the same order.

But everything Gilbert does is with the goal of becoming a better basketball player, and the results are there.

In his first season with the Wizards, Gilbert played just 55 games because of various injuries, but still averaged a career-high 19.6 points.

Last season, he started 80 games, increased his scoring average to 25.5 points, and averaged 5.1 assists.

He was not only selected to his first All-Star Game, but he helped the Wizards make the playoffs for the first time since the 1996–97 season and win a playoff series for the first time since 1981–82. No one knows what's next for Gilbert, but it's sure to be exciting.

Baron Davis

Growing up in Los Angeles, Baron Davis once believed he could never live anywhere but the West Coast. He went to college at UCLA in part because he didn't want to leave home.

But when he entered the NBA, Baron was no

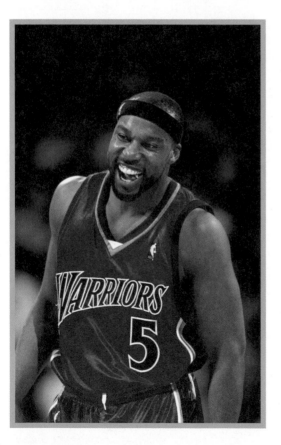

longer in control of his destiny. He would play for the Charlotte Hornets, who selected him as the No. 3 overall pick in 1999.

At first, Baron thrived with the Hornets, making two All-Star Game appearances, but then the franchise moved to New Orleans at the start of the 2003–04 season and things changed.

On February 24, 2005, Baron was traded to the Golden State Warriors. Due to various injuries, he had played just 18 games, and some people wondered if the Warriors had gotten damaged goods.

They had not. The Oakland/San Francisco Bay area may not be Los Angeles, but it is California, and Baron was rejuvenated. With the Warriors, Baron again became the dynamic point guard who had helped lead the Hornets to the playoffs in each of his first five seasons.

Baron's impact was dramatic. Before he arrived, the Warriors had won just 16 of their first 58 games. With Baron running the point, Golden State won 18 of its final 28 games, including a 14–4 stretch to close out the season. As a Warrior, Baron averaged 19.5 points and 8.3 assists, numbers that were similar to ones he had when he made the All-Star Game in 2002 and 2004.

To a franchise that hasn't made the playoffs in 11 seasons, Baron represents the hope for a brighter future and possibly a championship.

"I know I can play better," Baron said. "I can be quicker and stronger. If I'm quicker and stronger, I can play better."

And that can only be bad news for Baron's opponents.

Manu Ginobili

Growing up in the basketball-crazy city of Bahia Blanca, Argentina, Emmanuel "Manu" Ginobili did not see himself becoming an NBA Champion or All-Star.

He made his professional debut in Argentina when he was 18, and then two years later he signed with Basket Viola Reggio Calabria of the Italian League.

While Manu was starring in Italy, the San Antonio Spurs selected him with a late-second-round pick in the 1999 Draft, but Manu, who was the Italian League MVP in 2000–01 and 2001–02, did not sign

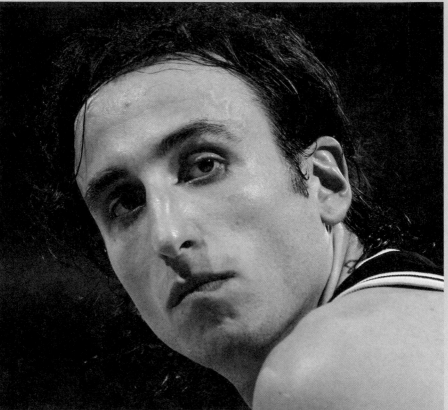

with the Spurs until the 2002–03 season.

He helped the Spurs win the 2003 NBA Championship during his rookie season and has improved in each of the following three seasons. He is now one of the top guards in the NBA.

In Argentina, Manu is a national hero, but not because he has two NBA Championship rings or because he made the 2005 All-Star Game. Manu has reached rock-star status because he has helped make Argentina's national basketball team into a world power just like its soccer team.

At the 2002 FIBA World Championships in Indianapolis, Argentina become the first country to defeat the United States since Team USA started using NBA players.

Then Manu led Argentina to its greatest international championship in basketball, as it defeated Italy in the gold medal game at the 2004 Olympics in Athens, Greece.

"I'm still playing and I started 6,000 miles from here," Manu said. "Every time I won something, I felt like I was in heaven."

It's a feeling Manu better get used to.

Ben Gordon

Ben Gordon was an All-State selection at Mount Vernon (N.Y.) High School before he went on to the University of Connecticut, which he helped lead to the 2004 NCAA Championship.

On NBA Draft night, he was selected third overall by the Chicago Bulls. But things weren't going the way Ben had anticipated. Despite the high draft selection, he couldn't crack the starting lineup. Ben could have let this become a real problem.

Instead of getting down, however, Ben, who ranked sixth on UConn's all-time scoring list (1,795 points) when he declared for the NBA

after his junior season, kept working hard and doing whatever his coaches wanted. His efforts are helping to make the Bulls a better team.

If that meant coming off the bench, then that was okay. "The way I was playing, I didn't deserve to be starting," said Ben, who was born in London and has a British passport. "I realized I had to find my niche."

And did he *ever*. Although he started just three of 82 games, Ben had as much impact as any player in helping Chicago return to the playoffs for the first time since 1998.

Ben averaged 15.1 points while playing 24.4 minutes a game. He also produced his biggest moments when it mattered the most in games. Ben scored 10 or more points in the fourth quarter of 21 games.

"He has come in this year and played with such poise and maturity," Bulls general manager John Paxson said of Ben. "It's very difficult for any rookie to come in and accept and acknowledge a role they are given, especially when it's one coming off the bench."

Because Ben was such a dynamic player coming off the bench, he became the first rookie ever to win the NBA's Sixth Man of the Year Award. More honors are bound to follow.

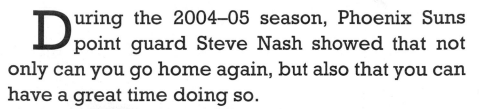

Steve Nash

During the 2004–05 season, Phoenix Suns point guard Steve Nash showed that not only can you go home again, but also that you can have a great time doing so.

In 1996, Nash, who grew up in British Columbia, Canada, was drafted 15th overall by the Suns out of Santa Clara University.

But early in Steve's rookie season, Phoenix acquired All-Star point guard Jason Kidd in a trade with the Dallas Mavericks. The next season, Steve was traded to Dallas, and he found himself starting over again. It wasn't surprising because Steve, who was born in South

Grant Hill

Who says nice guys have to finish last? Between 1994 and 2000, Grant Hill established himself as one of the best — and classiest — players in the NBA.

Selected third overall by the Detroit Pistons in the 1994 Draft, Grant was co-rookie of the year with Jason Kidd and then went on to make five All-Star Games.

He was First Team All-NBA in 1997 and Second Team four other times. In 1996 he won a gold medal with the United States at the Olympics.

He was one of the best players in the world. After the 1999–2000 season, the Pistons dealt Grant, who was a free agent, to the Orlando Magic in a sign-and-trade. He was supposed to pair up with free agent Tracy McGrady to make the Magic the team to beat in the Eastern Conference.

But Grant played just four games in his first season in Orlando. A devastating ankle injury would limit him to just 47 games over the next three seasons. He went through five ankle surgeries.

It looked like his career was over. Grant, however, never stopped working to get back, and

Grant Hill receives the 2004–05 NBA Sportsmanship Award from Hall of Famer Bob Lanier.

after 18 months of intense rehabilitation, he finally got back on the court last season. Playing in 67 games, he averaged 19.7 points, 4.7 rebounds, and 3.3 assists.

Grant, who is married to Grammy Award–nominated singer Tamia, was voted a starter to the 2005 Eastern Conference All-Star Team and was given the 2004–05 NBA Sportsmanship Award. This nice guy will definitely be making more appearances as an All-Star, and he should expect even higher honors.

Africa but grew up in Canada, has always had to prove himself.

"It seems like my whole life I've been this little Canadian kid dreaming that somebody would give me a chance," he said.

Steve, whose father, John, was a professional soccer player, played soccer after his junior year at St. Michael's University School. He was named British Columbia's most valuable player. He could have made the Canadian National Soccer Team.

But he loved basketball more. Both Steve and his high school coach believed he could play NCAA Division I basketball. They sent letters to two dozen schools, including Arizona, Duke, and Maryland. Only Santa Clara University, a small college near San Francisco, offered him a scholarship.

At Santa Clara, Steve was twice named West Coast Conference Player of the Year (in 1994–1995 and 1995–1996) and finished as the Broncos' all-time leader, with 510 assists. He was third on the all-time scoring list with 1,689 points.

In Dallas, Steve was a two-time All-Star, but the Mavericks let him sign a free-agent contract in Phoenix after the 2003–04 season.

Back with the Suns, Steve directed one of

the most amazing turnarounds in NBA history. Phoenix went from winning 29 games in 2003–04 to posting a league-best 62–20 record in 2004–05.

Averaging an NBA-best 11.5 assists and scoring 15.5 points a game, Steve became the first Canadian to be named NBA Most Valuable Player.

"I was never supposed to play in college, let alone the NBA, so I always feel like I have something to prove," Steve said. And he's going to keep on proving it, even if everyone else feels he has done it all.

Dirk Nowitzki

$\mathbf{M}$aybe if the "Dream Team" had never existed, Dallas Mavericks star Dirk Nowitzki would've kept playing soccer like most of the kids in his hometown of Wurzburg, Germany.

But after watching the 1992 United States Olympic Basketball team that featured Michael Jordan, Larry Bird, and Magic Johnson, 14-year-old Nowitzki knew he wanted to play basketball.

He worked to improve his skills, and it helped that by the time he had reached college age, Dirk was 7 feet tall. Rather than coming to America and playing in college, he played for DJK Wurzburg of the German Bundesliga.

Although there were stories about this kid in Germany, Dirk didn't catch the attention of NBA scouts until 1998, when he played in the Nike Hoops Summit in San Antonio.

He scored 33 points to lead a group of international junior players to a victory over the USA juniors.

Dirk entered the NBA Draft and was selected ninth overall by the Milwaukee Bucks, but he was traded immediately to the Mavericks for Robert "Tractor" Traylor.

For the better part of his first six seasons, Dirk has been the best player on the Dallas Mavericks. But the 2004–05 season provided another challenge when All-Star point guard Steve Nash went to Phoenix as a free agent. Dirk had to step up as the Mavericks' leader, not just their best player. Dirk was uncomfortable assuming the position of team leader, because that meant becoming more vocal and sometimes calling teammates out.

Still, he knew it was his responsibility and he grew into the role as the season went on. Dirk finished fourth in the league in scoring, averaging a career-high 26.1 points and 9.7 rebounds. But his evolution into a more complete player could not be ignored. Not only was Dirk selected to his fourth All-Star Game, but he also became the first Maverick ever to be named First Team All-NBA. Fans can be sure that it won't be the last time, either.

Emeka Okafor

There is always pressure on a rookie selected high in an NBA Draft. Usually the team making the pick is coming off a bad season, and the player taken is expected to help it get better.

Emeka Okafor was under an entirely different set of expectations. After he led the University

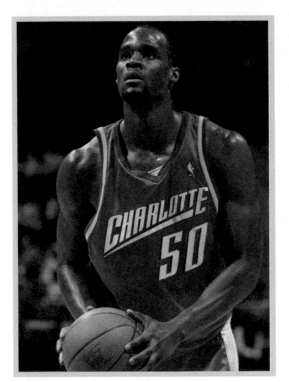

of Connecticut to the 2004 NCAA Championship and was named Most Outstanding Player of the Final Four, everyone knew that Emeka was going to be one of the top picks in the 2004 NBA Draft.

The expansion Charlotte Bobcats traded up to the number two overall

pick to make Emeka the cornerstone for building a new franchise.

"With an expansion team, I knew that things would be different," said Emeka, who played for the United States at the 2004 Olympics before starting his NBA career, "but I didn't have anything to compare it to. I can't complain at all. I've had a great time in Charlotte this year and it's only going to get better. The future is bright."

The Bobcats' future is bright because Emeka has lived up to the billing and was voted the NBA

Rookie of the Year. Emeka led all rookies in scoring (15.9 points a game) and rebounding (10.9 per game). He was second among rookies by averaging 1.71 blocks per game.

He was also fourth in the league with 47 double-doubles. But none of that is surprising. Emeka has been succeeding since he was a star at Bellaire High in Houston, Texas. In three seasons at UConn, he led the Huskies to an 83–23 record. He finished his college career averaging 13.7 points and 10.5 rebounds.

Although Emeka left school after his junior season, he had already graduated with a degree in finance. He was named to the 2003 and 2004 College Sports Information Directors Academic All-America First Team, and the 2004 Academic All-America of the Year for the University Division.

Given Emeka's drive and ability, Bobcats fans can expect a lot from their new star.

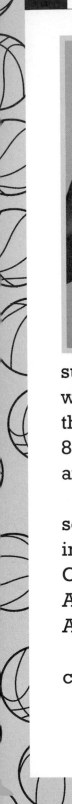

Dwyane Wade

It was hard for Miami Heat guard Dwyane Wade not to be overlooked his first two seasons in the NBA. Although he was selected fifth overall in the 2003 Draft, two of the players picked ahead of him — LeBron James and Carmelo Anthony — were some of the most celebrated rookies to enter the league in years.

Then, despite having a terrific first season averaging 16.2 points and 4.5 assists, Dwyane got a new teammate last summer who grabbed all of the attention again — Shaquille O'Neal.

But being lost in the shadows wasn't acceptable to Dwyane, who had led Marquette

University to the 2003 NCAA Final Four. He knew the best way to get noticed was to shine brightly on the court.

"My will is to always be better and better," said Dwyane, whose nickname is Flash. "I've got the will to want to be the best."

Before his NBA sophomore year began, Dwyane earned headlines helping the United States win the bronze medal at the 2004 Olympics in Athens.

Then when the season started, Dwyane showed just how much he had improved. He raised his scoring average from 16.2 points to 24.1 points and his assist average from 4.5 to 6.8. He was selected to his first NBA All-Star Team and was named Second Team All-NBA.

By the end of the season, Dwyane was being called one of the best players in the game. "Life is not measured by the number of breaths that you take but by the moments that you take breath away," Miami Heat president and Hall of Fame coach Pat Riley said. "That's what Dwyane is about."

Count on Dwyane Wade to leave a lot of people breathless.

Read to Achieve

This year, NBA Players and Coaches are continuing to share their words…

And by promoting reading and on-line literacy, they are spreading the word that every child should have the chance to *Read to Achieve*.

FOR MORE INFORMATION ON READ TO ACHIEVE, LOG ON TO NBA.com.